What's the Supreme Court?

Nancy Harris

Heinemann Library
Chicago, Illinois

©2008 Heinemann Library
a division of Reed Elsevier Inc.
Chicago, Illinois

Customer Service 888-454-2279
Visit our website at **www.heinemannlibrary.com**

Designed by Kimberly R. Miracle and Betsy Wernert
Photo Research by Tracy Cummins and Tracey Engel
Maps provided by Map Specialists
Printed in China by South China Printing Company

11 10 09
10 9 8 7 6 5 4 3 2

ISBN-10: 1-4034-9467-3 (hc)   1-4034-9473-8 (pb)

Library of Congress Cataloging-in-Publication Data
Harris, Nancy, 1956-
  What's the Supreme Court? / Nancy Harris.
     p. cm. -- (First guide to government)
  Includes bibliographical references and index.
  ISBN 978-1-4034-9467-2 (hc) -- ISBN 978-1-4034-9473-3 (pb)
  1. United States. Supreme Court--Juvenile literature. 2. Judicial power--United States--Juvenile literature. I. Title.
  KF8742.Z9H37 2007
  347.73'26--dc22
                              2007003265

Acknowledgments
The author and publishers are grateful to the following for permission to reproduce copyright material: AP Photo pp. **8** (Columbus
Dispatch, Tom Dodge), **12** (Ken Heinen), **15** (J. Scott Applewhite), **16** (Dana Verkouteren), **19** (Ken Hively, Pool), **24** (Charles
Dharapak), **26** (Dana Verkouteren); Collection of the Supreme Court of the United States pp. **21, 22, 23, 27**; Corbis pp. **4**
(Royalty-Free), **25** (Brooks Kraft), **28** (Bettmann); Getty Images pp. **6** (Jahi Chikwendiu-Pool), **7** (AFP/CHARLIE ARCHAMBAULT),
9 (AFP/BETH KEISER), **10** (Newsmakers/Chris Hondros), **14** (Mark Wilson), **17** (David Hume Kennerly), **18** (Bill Pugliano), **29**
(The Image Bank/Dave Nagel); National Archives p. **13**; Reuters p. **20**.

Cover photograph reproduced with permission of Hisham Ibrahim/Photov.com/Alamy.

Disclaimer
All the Internet addresses (URLs) given in this book were valid at the time of going to press. However, due to the dynamic nature of
the Internet, some addresses may have changed, or sites may have changed or ceased to exist since publication. While the author
and publisher regret any inconvenience this may cause readers, no responsibility for any such changes can be accepted by either the
author or the publisher.

Contents

Some words are shown in bold, **like this**. You can find out what they mean by looking in the glossary.

What Is the Supreme Court?

The Supreme Court is part of the United States **federal government**. The federal government runs the whole country.

★ The Supreme Court is in Washington, D.C.

The federal government is made up of three branches (parts). Each part has a special job. One of the branches is called the **judicial branch**. The Supreme Court is part of this branch.

The Judicial Branch

★★★ People in the judicial branch decide if a person or group has broken a law.

The job of the **judicial branch** is to make sure the **laws** (rules) are understood. People who work in the judicial branch decide if a law has been broken.

judge

lawyer

The main people who work in the judicial branch are:

- **judges**
- **lawyers.**

★ Judges listen to people talk before they make a decision.

A **judge** is a person who knows the **laws**. Judges work in **courts**. A court is a place people go to if they feel a law has been broken. The judge decides if the law has been broken.

A **lawyer** is a person who knows the laws. Lawyers help people who go to court. They talk to the judge for the person. They try to get the judge to agree with that person's opinion.

★ Lawyers talk with judges about the law.

These talks are called cases. Each case involves talking about a specific **law** or laws. A case can last days or even months. The case usually ends with a decision about whether the law has been broken.

★★★ The Supreme Court makes decisions about important cases.

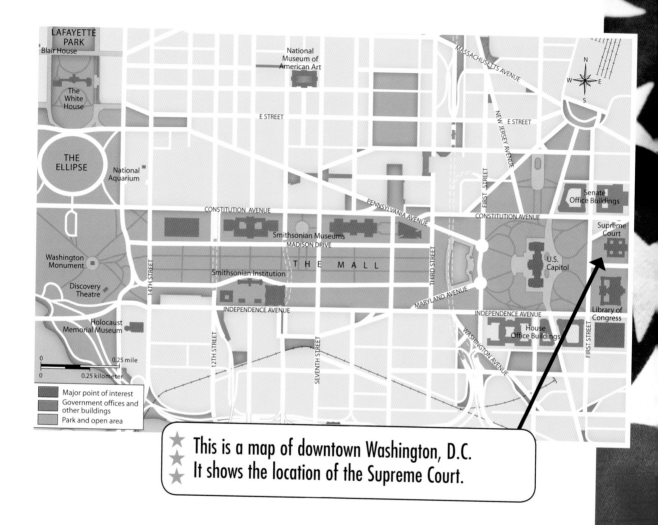

This is a map of downtown Washington, D.C. It shows the location of the Supreme Court.

Cases take place in **courts**. There are many courts in the **judicial branch**. The Supreme Court is the highest court. It is in Washington, D.C., the capital of the United States.

The Job of the Supreme Court

The Supreme Court is the most powerful **court** in the country. Supreme Court **judges** make sure the **law** of the **United States Constitution** is followed.

★ Supreme Court judges have a very important job.

The Constitution describes how the three branches of government work together. The Constitution must be followed by everyone in the United States.

★ The Constitution went into effect on March 4, 1789.

★★★ This is a photograph of people in the legislative branch meeting together.

The Supreme Court makes decisions about the actions of the other branches of the **federal government**. They can decide if these branches are following the **law** of the **United States Constitution**.

★ People in the legislative branch work in the Capitol building.

The Supreme Court hears cases about **federal laws**. Federal laws are made by people in the **legislative branch**. The legislative branch is part of the federal government.

Federal laws must follow the **law** of the **United States Constitution**. Supreme Court **judges** decide whether federal laws follow these rules.

The Supreme Court usually listens to cases involving Constitutional law or federal laws.

Supreme Court judges use the Constitution to make a decision about a case. They also use decisions from past Supreme Court cases to support their decision.

How Does a Case Get to the Supreme Court?

★ Lower courts hear more cases than the Supreme Court.

Most cases do not go to the Supreme Court. They are heard in lower **courts**. Every state has many lower courts.

Judges in the lower courts make a decision on a case. They decide if a **law** has been broken.

★★★ Judges read many papers about a case before they make a decision.

Sometimes people do not agree with a lower **court's** decision. They can then bring their case to another court. If the case is important enough, it goes to the Supreme Court.

★ People can visit the Supreme Court.

Judges on the Supreme Court decide if they will hear the case. Few cases are heard by the Supreme Court.

★★★ This is the room where Supreme Court judges meet to discuss cases.

Supreme Court Judges

There are nine **judges** on the Supreme Court today. These judges make decisions about **laws** that affect the whole country.

★ These are the Supreme Court judges that serve today.

★★★ John Roberts is the chief justice. He is the leader of the Supreme Court judges.

The head of the nine judges is called the **chief justice**. The other eight judges are called **associate justices**. Each person must be chosen to be a judge (justice).

★★★ President Bush chose Samuel Alito to be a Supreme Court justice.

The justices are first chosen by the president of the United States. Then people in the **Senate** vote on the president's choice. The Senate is part of the **legislative branch**.

If people in the Senate vote in favor of the president's choice, the person becomes a Supreme Court justice. The person can be a Supreme Court **judge** for as long as he or she likes.

★★★ Senators met with Samuel Alito. Then they voted for him to become a Supreme Court justice.

Justices listen to a case together. Then they vote to decide if a **law** has been broken. More than half of the justices must agree on the decision.

★★★ Supreme Court justices listen to **lawyers** present an argument for their case.

One of the justices writes a report about the decision. Sometimes the report says that a **federal law** should be changed.

★ A justice writes a report to explain the Supreme Court's decision.

Supreme Court Cases

★★★ *Brown v. Board of Education* was one of the most important Supreme Court cases in history.

The Supreme Court has heard many important cases. One famous case is *Brown v. Board of Education*. The Supreme Court ruled that it was against the **law** to have separate schools for black and white children. It decided all children should attend the same school.

Supreme Court decisions are very important. They can change the way things happen in the country.

★ Today all children can go to school together.

Glossary

associate justice Supreme Court judge

chief justice head judge of the Supreme Court

court place people can go if they feel a law has been broken

federal government group of leaders who run the entire country. In a federal government, the country is made up of many states.

federal law law that everyone in the United States must follow

judge person who knows the law. A judge works in a court. A judge decides if a law has been understood or if it has been broken.

judicial branch part of the United States federal government. This branch makes sure the laws (rules) are understood.

law rule people must obey in a state or country

lawyer person who knows the law. Lawyers help people who go to court. They try to get the judge to agree with that person's opinion.

legislative branch part of the United States federal government. This branch makes laws (rules). Congress is the legislative branch.

Senate house (group) in Congress where two people from each state work

United States Constitution written law telling how the three branches (parts) of the United States federal government must work

More Books to Read

An older reader can help you with these books:

January, Brendan. *The Supreme Court*. New York: Scholastic
    Library, 2004.

Murphy, Patricia J. *The U.S. Supreme Court*. Mankato, MN:
    Redbrick Learning, 2002.

Web Sites

Ben's Guide to Government (http://bensguide.gpo.gov/) gives young
readers information about how the United States government works.

Visiting the Supreme Court

You can visit the Supreme Court Monday through Friday from 9 am to 4:30 pm.

The Supreme Court address is:
Supreme Court of the United States
One First Street N.E.
Washington, DC 20543

Index